growing pains

caitlin brooke

ISBN: 978-1-914275-91-3

Perspective Press Global Ltd

to the broken
from the healed

the following pages detail my journey through young love, heartbreak, healing, and regaining faith in love. i wrote this book not just for myself, but also for you. i hope that you can find comfort in these words and begin the journey of healing any untreated wounds. most importantly, i hope you realise that feelings of heartbreak and loss are universal. you are never alone in this journey. please feel free to write in the empty spaces and make yourself at home.

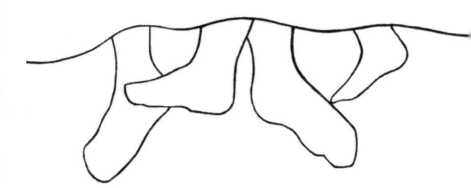

he was like a bad dream unfolding in front of your eyes
you feel helpless and alone, with no control
screaming into the void, searching for help
trying to save the one person who made life worth living

he was drowning
in his own insecurities
and became the anchor
that dragged her down

- *hurt people hurt people*

you told me you loved me
little did i know
this was the first
in a series of lies
that were about to blossom
how foolish of me to assume
there is only one wave in a set

you taught me that love
is a game of tug of war

constantly pulling at each other
until one of us falls down

your force would come and go in waves
so subtle, i didn't notice the signs
but now the waves are more frequent
and have grown in strength and size
i find myself losing breath
as i slip under the rising tide

i am tired of buying a new vase
every time your anger peaks
and you decide
it is no longer good enough
glass shatters
water disperses
flowers wither
along with my sense of security
i gather fragments of glass
and shrivelled petals
with a piece of newspaper
throw them away
and replace the flowers
in hopes of creating
a disguised sense of beauty
in this broken home,
but every time someone comments
on the beauty of the flowers
and the way their soft scent
spreads to every corner of the room
i am reminded of why
i had to buy them in the first place
i am reminded of why
this house is not a home
i am reminded of why
fear runs through my veins
every second of every day
but i smile through gritted teeth
"thank you, i bought them on tuesday"

my nightgown
frayed at the seam
ripped in places
you have been

white sheets
crumpled and torn
splashed with red wine
tainted by your lies

the body remembers
what my mind cannot
bruises on my neck,
pain or maybe pleasure

petals pulled off
one by one
scattered across
the cold timber floor

shivering in silence
drowning in deception
fighting the battle
my heart ignores

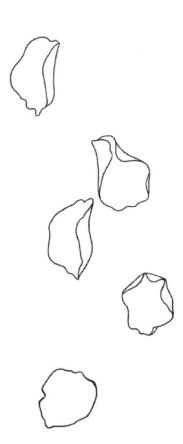

my fragile spine slides down
the newly painted wall
shivering in fear
frozen in my tracks

scared that these waterfalls
have erased my attempts
to cover the blues
of last night's argument

wearing an oversized cardigan
that just conceals the nail marks
engraved in my palms, my new
coping mechanism for pain

you see, those are the repercussions of
my oblivion.
my love.
you.

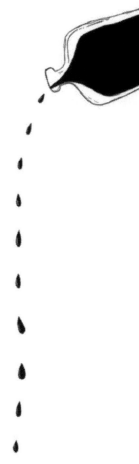

your love is a toxic addiction
like poison trickling down my throat
leaving just enough room for air
whilst slowly decaying my heart

-    *somebody get me the antidote*

you are just pawn in his game
sitting around waiting for him
to control your next move

little does he know
that once the queen falls
the king will crumble on his own

he was the leader of the kingdom
treating women like property
forcing them to bow down on their knees
before all his power and glory

one after another, women line up
believing this is the best life has to offer
waiting to kiss the feet of a man
who walks through dirt every day

with rope marks engraved in their wrists
purple stains on their knees
and fear in their eyes
they shuffle towards the throne

just another body in the sea of women
who are withered from the drought
of being overlooked by men
who think a crown determines their power

every time you forgive his actions
you make him think it's okay
to keep treating you that way
he will abuse your loyalty
and keep you wrapped around his finger
while he continues to handle you like dirt

in their lies
was everything
you wanted to hear
feeding the insecurities
buried deep in your soul
making you colour blind
to their red flags

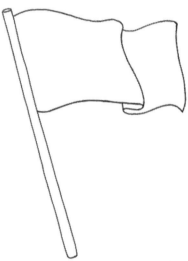

when will you learn
that words won't
heal your wounds?

i focused so much on trying to fix you
that i became blind to my own cracks

if i loved myself
then maybe i wouldn't fall
for a boy, so troubled and
drowning in his own flood

we teach young girls
to love bad boys
and are then surprised
when women fall
for toxic men

walking away from a toxic relationship
is one of the hardest things you will ever have to do
it is easy to only remember them for the good
but if you do not cut ties with those
you are trying to forget, their poison
will seep through the rope around your wrists

too often, i choose
toxic familiarity
over a fresh start
in fear of being hurt
by someone new
and settle for the pain
i already know

better the devil you know than the devil you don't

caitlin brooke – growing pains

you pushed me away
then accused me of leaving
and somehow you don't see the irony

you leave
but never stay gone
held prisoner in a love
full of empty promises
and pretend goodbyes,
will i ever escape?

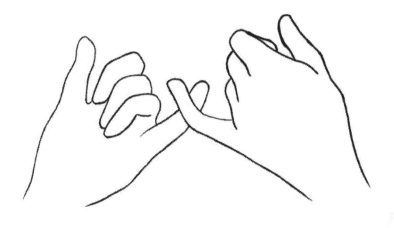

the moment i stopped loving myself
was when you convinced me
that no one else ever would

my mind often feels like a warzone, flooded with self-criticism and doubt. convincing myself that i will never live up to the unrealistic beauty standards our society has created. the more i fixate on my flaws, the deeper i dig myself into the trenches. suddenly, i am creating pointless conflict and wondering how i am going to survive. what they don't tell you is that if you are constantly at battle with yourself, you are doomed to lose the war to your own thoughts.

she is a lost soul, trying on a new guy each week
sick of the old, craving something new
wasting time on things she will never need
an unhealthy addiction that has her falling apart at the seam

when will she learn
that you cannot stitch
a broken heart?

i have been running on empty for a while now, convincing myself that the late nights and hangovers will be worth it if i can just find someone to spend my days with. but i sit here, alone on the bathroom floor, drowning in vodka. everything feels backwards. it took reaching rock bottom to realise that you need to fill up your own cup before you can start giving love to anyone else. at the end of the day, trying to pour love from an empty cup will just leave you both thirsty for more.

she was made of glass
so fragile and transparent
easily broken
at the touch of a hand
or a damaged heart

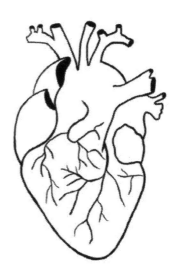

caitlin brooke – growing pains

i spent last night
lost in my own thoughts
wandering around in the realm
of what ifs and possibilities
hiding from the reality of heartbreak
creating impossible scenarios in my head
and breaking my own heart
rather than falling for a boy
who would do the exact same thing

she was mature for her age
intelligent and independent
with an outlook on the world
beyond her years, but in reality
she was forced to grow up too fast
coping with responsibilities
that well exceeded the standard
for a 16-year-old girl
they wonder why she is drowning
in trust issues and failed relationships
when she was stripped of her childhood
and any sense of normality

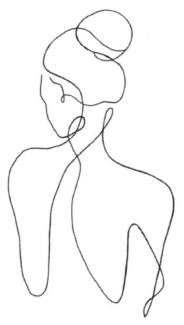

caitlin brooke – growing pains

you surround yourself
with people who weigh you down
and wonder why you're gasping for air

being aware of my own darkness
only digs me deeper into the black hole
as thoughts race through my mind
i know they're absurd, but i just
have no idea how to save myself

it's hard to see the light
when you are trapped
inside a black hole

waves crash over my head
as saltwater seeps into my wounds
finding peace in the silence
as i drift six feet under water
and ignore every life raft
hoping to drown in something
other than my own thoughts

every time she tried
to love someone new
she held herself back
in fear of falling
for the same old tricks
performed by a different boy

in fear of being alone
we find comfort in temporary bodies
running from our feelings
using shots of tequila
to fill the void
they left in our hearts

i wanted to love you
but i rushed into something
my heart was not ready for
you were a boy
who finally ticked all the boxes
but i couldn't give you
the love you deserved

- *give your wounds time to heal*

telling someone
you love them
when you don't
only makes it harder
to tell someone
you love them
when you do

there is something about you
that makes me feel alive
i know this is wrong
but i can't help it
you seem like everything
he could never be

- *maybe there is hope after all*

after years of hesitation
we have finally crossed a line
that we cannot retrace

can we ever go back
to being just friends?

i still remember
the first time we kissed
like it was yesterday
your hands in my hair
my arms around your neck
the kind of moment
that almost makes you sad
because nothing in this lifetime
could ever be so perfect

i have always craved this kind of love
the type that makes my heart race
sends butterflies through my stomach
and keeps me up at night
maybe that is where i am going wrong
because a spark can only last so long
before it fades, and all you have left
is your commitment to each other

caitlin brooke – growing pains

two naive souls
walking blindly into the abyss
searching for hope amongst
the chaos of young love

two lost souls
running in circles
drowning in infatuation
drifting further from reality

two young souls
falling in and out of love
hoping that one day this push and pull
will fill the void in their hearts

young love isn't all they make it out to be. something that is supposed to be pure and innocent can quickly turn into childish games. somehow, it has become very easy to fall into the same trap over and over again. so i sit here in silence, hold my breath, and try to ignore this sinking feeling in my stomach as i watch yet another boy try to pull the same tricks.

the way we talk about love bewilders me
growing up we believe it is better than life itself
with picture-perfect romance on the screen
and parents who couldn't be happier

suddenly we are taught phrases like
falling in love
breaking hearts
a *crush*
and somehow, we are still meant to have faith in love

- *maybe we were doomed from the start*

you have to remember that
just because he didn't love you
in the way that you wanted
doesn't mean he didn't love you
with everything that he had

my biggest fear is that one day
you will see me the way i see myself

caitlin brooke – growing pains

lately, we have grown apart
like two ships passing in the night
how many missed calls and pointless arguments
before we push each other overboard?

happiness may come in waves
but his love for you never should

watching someone fall out of love with you
is the cruellest form of heartbreak
that we as humans can experience

young love, so naive
falling into the same trap
over and over again
drowning in my hopes
that a boy like you
could fix a girl like me
in reality, i became so consumed
by trying to make you fall in love with me
that i forgot why i even loved myself
and after weeks of attention and late-night calls
your love grew less and less frequent
as the waves roar faded to a lull
and all that was left
were my bare feet stuck in the sand
that is when i finally realised
that if someone really wanted to stay
nothing could ever make them leave

the cards were stacked against me
and still i went all in
gambling everything for a boy
who was only bluffing

- *love is a losing game*

fight for someone who loves you
but never fight for someone to love you

in fear of losing people
we often hold on too tight
and end up suffocating
the ones we love most

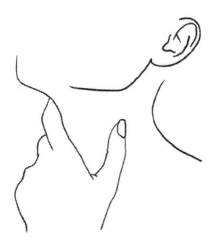

i didn't realise how quickly
we went from lovers to strangers
until i was staring at the arms
i used to call home
that are now covered in ink
from another life
we once shared everything
now strangers who know too much
too important to each other to let go
too damaged to look each other in the eye

there were often days that i could not get out of bed. the
heartbreak of losing you weighed so heavily on my heart that
i couldn't fathom moving my body. i soon realised that i was
never going to move on with my life if i didn't put one foot in
front of the other. but please remember to show yourself
some patience. sometimes it can take your heart a little while
to understand what your head already knows.

the heartbreak of losing you
was just like lemon juice
seeping into a fresh wound
leaving a burn that feels everlasting
you just have to remind yourself
that like every other pain
this too shall pass

i watched you get over me
by getting under her
you made it look so easy
but she was just good for your ego
easy on the eyes, sweet like honey
the girl that everyone wanted
to check off their list

i don't want her
to know you
like i know you
i know it's selfish
but even though
you aren't mine
the thought of you
with someone else
sends shivers
down my spine

one day,
you will look back
at the woman you loved
and she will be holding
the hand of someone
who is twice the man
you will ever be
because you may have made
flowers bloom in her lungs
and although they were beautiful
she couldn't breathe

weak men
always crawl back
when you are happier
with someone new

you are not allowed to miss me
when you are the one who threw me away
your absence taught me
to find strength in solitude
so, i am no longer the girl
who will wait on your every need
but you are still the man
who was always halfway out the door

the possibility of a future with you has always stopped me from falling in love with anyone else. i held so tightly onto any last string of false hope you fed me that it almost burnt me to shreds. i grew so naive to the fact that you were using me, that i would have done anything to make you stay. but the truth is, you always put me back on the shelf whenever you no longer needed me, left alone to collect dust. the longer i stayed wrapped around your finger, the less i recognised myself. that is the scariest place to be, because a part of me will always belong to you. if only i could find the girl i was before you broke my heart.

caitlin brooke – growing pains

i lost myself in you
and i have been trying
to find her ever since
but that chapter is closed
and she in nowhere to be seen
maybe this is for the best

caitlin brooke – growing pains

falling in love with someone
who doesn't have the same heart as you
will just push you further underwater

ever since you broke my heart
i have been trying to put
the pieces back together
it's been three years
and this glue still won't stick

out of everyone in my life
i never thought you would be temporary

caitlin brooke – growing pains

i am in love with a version of you that no longer exists
constantly creating fairy tales in my head
trying to ignore the fact that we are not the same kids
who met on penrose lane, the problem is
i don't think i will ever love anyone as much as i love(d) you
and i have no idea how to grieve the death
of someone who is still alive

i don't want to forgive you
i put my heart on the line
just for you to walk all over it
a lifetime has passed, and still
i see your footprints everyday
slowly fading, but never gone

-   *how do i erase you?*

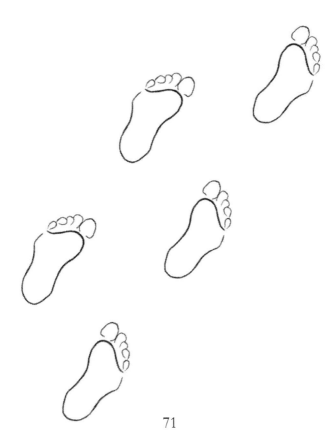

71

everyone else is a tourist
unable to break down the walls
i built around his heart

- *his first love*

your next lover
will trace the outline
my fingertips engraved
in your skin, hoping that
one day she could erase
your memory of my touch
but my imprint is permanent
and you will never forget
the way i loved you

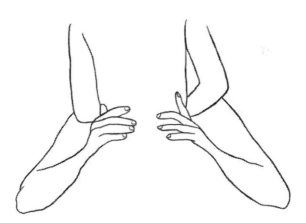

they say time is the cure for heartbreak
but no matter how many years have passed
seeing you again is like losing my place in a book
so easily picking up right back where we left off
and falling in love all over again

caitlin brooke – growing pains

if you told me you still loved me
all self-control would go out the window
and i would run back to everything that tore me to shreds

almost

/ˈɔːlməʊst/

adverb

the most heart-breaking word
in the english language

i often wonder if there will ever be a day
that you don't cross my mind
once i have bleached you from existence
and your absence is no longer left
once i have overcome the pain
of never having a proper goodbye
but for now, you walk through my mind every day
acting like you didn't drag me through hell

- *will i ever get over you?*

i still see you in my dreams
a soulmate who wasn't meant to be
haunted by the things we never said
running from the things we could never be

- *the one that got away*

my days are consumed
with overwhelming anxiety
running from the truth
that no one will ever
make me feel the way you do

i would have given you everything
but our love was always a waiting game
and as each soft kiss
slowly fades from my memory
i am learning to love you from a distance

my whole life, i thought it would be us in the end
that our different paths would eventually cross
but the truth is, you left my life a long time ago
and i am in love with who we used to be
scared of what will happen when
i finally let go of the idea of you and me

- *who do you blame when you break your own heart?*

on cold rainy days, i like to read through our story
flicking through pages of the past
reminiscing on a love that only existed in my head

you were always my favourite chapter, but lately
i have been struggling to get you out of my head
how am i meant to get closure when we never put pen to
paper?

everything still reminds me of you
whether it's cold coffee in the morning
or driving late with the windows down
there are remnants of you
scattered through my reality
and i can only hope that one day
every last piece of you
evaporates from existence

caitlin brooke – growing pains

i have always loved the idea of you
hoping that one day our fiction would become reality
but not getting what you so desperately want
can sometimes be a blessing in disguise

- *it's time to change the story*

it took me a really long time to realise
that i couldn't mourn the loss of you
because i still had hope you would change
and the fairy tale i had always dreamed of
would come true, but it is time
to finally take off the rose-tinted glasses
and see him for who he truly is
a man who took advantage of my love
and was never really mine to begin with

every now and then, i like to walk down memory lane
reminiscing on sunday mornings spent in bed
devouring pancakes as sunlight glistens through the window

the sound of jack johnson vibrating around the room
as we spray whipped cream into each other's mouths
and take polaroids to capture the moment

time has shown me that life is full of small moments like this
and it's okay if they don't last forever
because they will always be a part of our story

i often struggle
to write about
the happy moments
maybe that is why
i crave sadness
maybe that is why
i put my heart
in positions
to get crushed
it fuels the fire
of my poetry

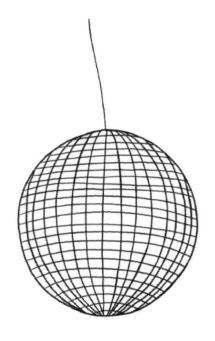

and just like a disco ball
she was so broken
yet somehow allowed others to shine
that is how you know
she is one of a kind
that is how you know
you should never let her go

she was addicted to the darkness
chasing things that didn't belong to her
falling in love with stolen hearts
searching for validation in anyone but herself

when is she going to start
taking her own advice
and turn this pain
into something beautiful

how many times
do you need to hurt
before you realise
that love *doesn't*

the most beautiful artworks
are drawn by people
who are a little broken
on the inside

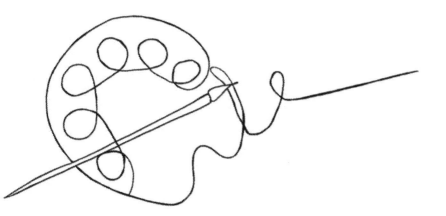

it is time to take everything
you were willing to give them
and give it to yourself

caitlin brooke – growing pains

you need to let him go
and give up the fantasy
of what could have been
in order to write your own story
because if i am being honest
letting go is much easier
than holding on to something
that was never real

set yourself free

the most heart-breaking lesson i have learned is that just because you loved each other does not mean you were meant to be. not everyone is supposed to be in your life forever. sometimes people come into your life for a short period of time. we can either focus on the fact that we are experiencing a loss or remind ourselves that every time your heart breaks, sunflowers will grow through the cracks.

trying to walk away
and hold on
at the same time
will tear you apart
so my darling, learn to
break out of your comfort zone
find strength in solitude
and most importantly, do not
allow people to mistreat you
just because you are not ready
to let them go

i have never been good with losing people. i spend my days trying to erase any remnants of their existence. but no matter how hard i try, i can never seem to shake the imprint they left on my life. i am stuck between wanting to move on and create a life without them, and being terrified of finally letting go. the older i get, the more i realise that people come and go. just because you need to let them go, does not mean you need to erase everything about them. you have the opportunity to learn something valuable from every relationship you have throughout your life. erasing their memories only robs you of this chance to learn more about yourself and the world you live in. at the end of the day, if someone isn't willing to fight for you, you have to be smart enough to walk away. the only real constant is you. that is the relationship that is worth nourishing. that is the love you need to focus on.

choose people that choose you

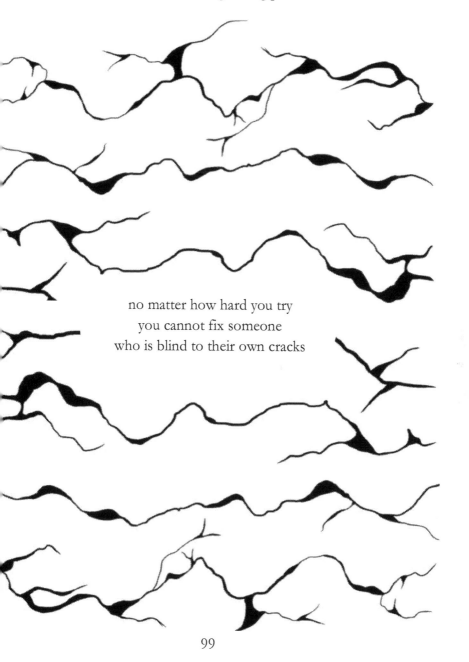

no matter how hard you try
you cannot fix someone
who is blind to their own cracks

i think it is time to finally let you go
because you may need me, but i need myself more
after all, how am i supposed to plant new seeds
if i continue watering a dead plant

there are many times in life
that you will find yourself
standing at a crossroads
between turning the page
and closing the book
i can tell you from experience
that you will never get
the closure you need
by just turning the page

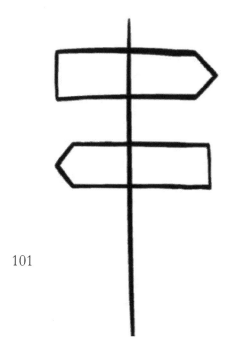

it was a pleasure to call you mine
but now i have to go, because you were just
a temporary band aid for my heart
and i need to fix what is underneath

caitlin brooke – growing pains

to know the heartbreak of losing you
means i had the pleasure of being loved by you
and i am okay with that

it takes a strong person to understand that while they didn't deserve what they went through, they also wouldn't be where they are today without that pain

one day you will wake up
to a vase on the dining room table
filled with a beautiful bouquet
and those who took advantage
of your patience and mercy
will just be a distant memory
you will learn to never wait
for any man to buy you flowers
and instead spend each and every day
building your own garden

happiness. it's a crazy thing. for so long i have been striving for a constant state of happiness. to never have bad days. to never feel insecure. to never cry. to never doubt myself. the list goes on. but this is impossible. being happy isn't about never feeling sad. it's knowing that bad days will come, and bad days will go. it's knowing that good days are right around the corner. it's knowing that insecurities are normal. it's knowing that having an emotional outlet does not make you weak. it's knowing all of these things and still being content with the person you are. this is so much more important than an unattainable, unrealistic constant state of happiness.

the most valuable advice i have ever received is to honour
your season. it is so easy to fall into the trap of doing things
that are expected of us. we are constantly flooded with the
highlight reels of everyone around us, reaching milestones
that we are 'supposed' to be chasing. at the end of the day, if
we spend so much time caught up in the achievements of
others, we will never truly live a single day in our own lives.
all we can do is focus on where we are now, and take small
steps every day to build the life we want to live.

we spend so much time caught up in making the right decisions. creating pro con lists till our fingers bleed. having many sleepless nights running around in circles, overthinking every possible outcome. spending too much time caught in indecision that we forget to be present each and every day. the truth is, there is no 'right' decision. all you can do is trust your gut and not let the pressure of making the right choice eat up at your precious time on this earth.

my life changed when i decided to let go of what i thought it was supposed to look like. at the end of the day, some of the greatest stories have a plot twist.

the hardest lesson i ever had to learn
was that in order to grow
you have to cull the weeds

and just like the moon
we have to experience
phases of emptiness
before we can be whole again

caitlin brooke – growing pains

i held my own hand
cried on my own shoulder
wiped away my own tears
and picked myself back up
that is when i learnt
that all the strength
i could ever need
was growing within me

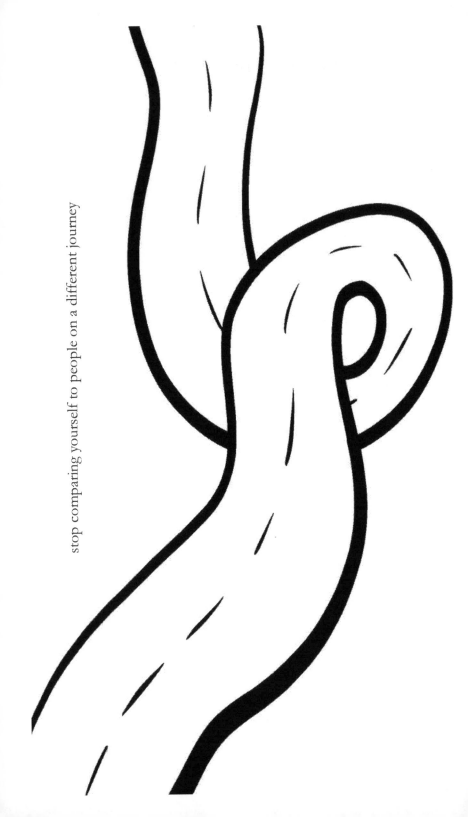

stop comparing yourself to people on a different journey

thank you for not loving me
it forced me to love myself

we live in a world that rates beauty on a scale from 1 to 10
creating insecurities we didn't know we had
picking out our flaws and comparing us to an ideal
forcing us to seek validation from others
when in reality, our true beauty comes from within

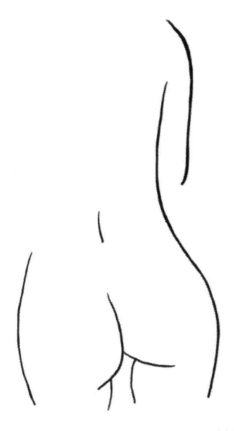

caitlin brooke – growing pains

when people make you feel
like you are not enough
it often has nothing to do with you
the phrase 'hurt people hurt people'
wasn't coined out of nowhere
because in order for someone
to cause people pain
they must be in pain themselves

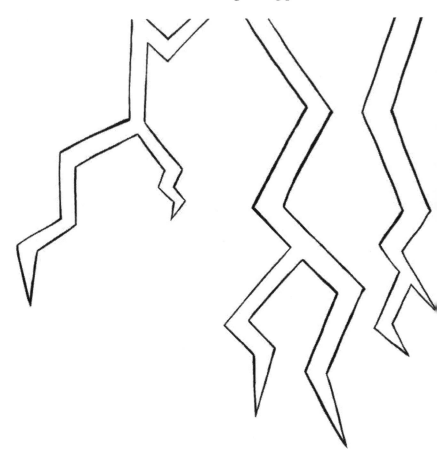

you were built to survive the storm

you owe yourself an apology,
for all the times you let someone walk all over you
for all the times you didn't ask for help
for all the times you didn't stand up for yourself
for all the times you lost yourself looking for love
for all the times you blamed yourself for the heartache
but most of all, for all the times you didn't love yourself

you will eventually come to realise
that friends can break your heart too
as they start accusing you of changing
when all you did was outgrow them

- *growing pains*

we are so fixated on reaching new heights
that we forget how far we have already climbed

you will soon realise
that even though
you never would have
pulled the trigger
ending this relationship
was the best thing
to ever happen to you

distance yourself from people
who make you feel hard to love

the concept of someone
being your other half
gives this false impression
that we are not whole on our own

going out into the world
on your own is daunting
but the only way
you are ever going to fly
is if you leave the nest

you are not responsible
for the version of you
they created in their head
the only thing you can control
is your state of mind

-   *rise above*

if you water your own garden
it will never matter
how green the grass is
on the other side

it takes strength
to practise kindness
in the face of evil

caitlin brooke – growing pains

if you have the courage
to trust love one more time
it might just surprise you

timing has never been our strong suit
floating in and out of other relationships
and breaking our own hearts
maybe it was meant to be this way
we had to experience heartbreak
in order to appreciate the love
we can give each other
in order to know
what we deserve
in order to understand
that we couldn't be
more right for each other

this is a different kind of love
reading second-hand books in the coffee shop kind of love
flipping through old records in the vintage store kind of love
holding hands in the hallways of the library kind of love
kissing in the back corner of the art museum kind of love
the kind of love that people dream of
the kind of love that makes time stand still
the kind of love you will never forget

for so long,
i have had concrete walls
built around my heart
that no one could cross
many tried, many failed
then *you* came along
with your sweet chocolate eyes
knocked each brick down
peeled back the layers of my skin
took my heart in your hands
and taught me how to love again

if you don't have the capacity
to work on yourself while in a relationship
you aren't dating the right person
because anyone who truly loves you
whether that has been for three weeks or ten years
should always want what is best for you

i have always wished for a love like this
every time i blew out my birthday candles
or found a dandelion in my back yard
a love that makes you feel safe
a love that feels like home

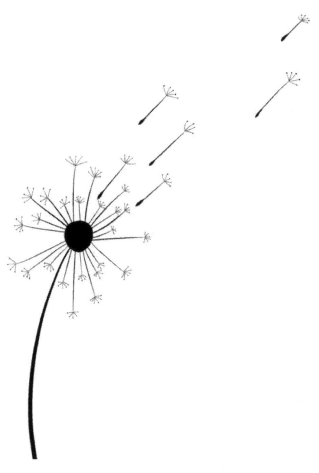

our love makes me feel safe
and just like the sun
which rises and sets
each and every day
i find comfort in knowing
it is always going to be there

too many sleepless nights
spent tossing and turning
homesick for your touch
counting the days until our stars align
and you are back by my side

- *long distance*

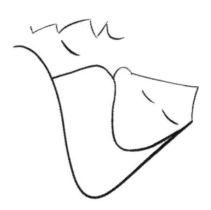

loving you has taught me
that there can be peace
in the middle of the storm

i am here to remind you
that despite the storm
you will survive

i am here to remind you
that despite the chaos
you will find yourself again

i am here to remind you
that despite the heartache
you will find love again

i am here to remind you
that flowers can grow
in the darkest places

caitlin brooke – growing pains

poetry is a way of survival
healing the heart of untold stories
bleeding onto the pages
emptying your soul of past trauma
so that you too can begin to rebuild

- *this is why i write*

ISBN: 978-1-914275-91-3

Perspective Press Global Ltd

About The Author

Caitlin Brooke is a 22-year-old girl from New South Wales Australia. From a young age, she quickly realised the power poetry had and it became a passion.

Writing soon became a safe space for Caitlin during some of her darkest times. By sharing her writing and illustrations with the world, she hopes she can create that safe space for everyone else.

This is Caitlin's first published collection, and this book was inspired by her own journey through young love and heartbreak. This book contains everything she wished she could have known along her healing journey.

About The Publisher

Perspective Press Global is an independent publishing firm representing predominantly authors under the age of 20. Each summer we open our submissions for those above 20!

At Perspective Press Global, our mission is to inspire young aspiring authors that there is no such thing as being 'too young;' your voices deserve to be heard.

The firm was founded by Eleni Sophia as she struggled to find representation when she was a 13-year-old writer. We now have published young talent from around the globe – including, the UK, Albania, Australia, Ireland, and Kosovo!

If you're interested in joining our team, please visit our submissions page at perspectivepressglobal.com and come say hello over on Instagram @PerspectivePressGlobal